A VOTE FOR SUSANNA

THE FIRST WOMAN MAYOR

Karen M. Greenwald
illustrated by Sian James

Albert Whitman & Company
Chicago, Illinois

To my parents, my heroes,
Paula and Andrew Greenwald—
you own my heart—KMG

To Mum and Dad—SJ

Library of Congress Cataloging-in-Publication data is on file with the publisher.
Text copyright © 2021 by Karen M. Greenwald
Illustrations copyright © 2021 by Albert Whitman & Company
Illustrations by Sian James
First published in the United States of America in 2021 by Albert Whitman & Company
ISBN 978-0-8075-5313-8 (hardcover)
ISBN 978-0-8075-5314-5 (ebook)
Printed in China
10 9 8 7 6 5 4 3 2 1 RRD 26 25 24 23 22 21

Design by Rick DeMonico

For more information about Albert Whitman & Company,
visit our website at www.albertwhitman.com.

March 2, 1934, Norman, Oklahoma

Dora made her grandson an extraordinary promise. One she never made for anyone before.

On Dora's birthday this year, Ed could help her bake her famous angel food cake. He felt so proud. Grandma picked *him* to help!

But sharing her secret recipe wouldn't be Dora's only surprise that day.

That morning, Dora called out ingredients. "Eggs, sugar, salt, flour..."
Ed fidgeted with his apron.

"Is something wrong, darling?" she asked.

He whispered so softly she had to bend her head to hear.

"I want to help, but my friends said only girls bake."

"So...your friends know what boys *can't* do. Do you want to hear a story about a girl who was told what she *couldn't* do?"
He nodded.

"In 1887 a young woman named Susanna lived in the tiny city of Argonia, Kansas."

"Grandma, that's a loooong time ago!"

She chuckled. "Forty-seven years ago!"

Back then the law said Susanna couldn't do many of the things her brothers did.

Women in the United States couldn't vote. They couldn't write laws. But they had to follow them.

Men voted.
Men wrote laws.
Men had all the rights.

"One day in 1887," Dora told Ed, "Kansas passed a new law. It gave women residents a teeny taste of the rights men always enjoyed. Women could now vote and run for office in their own cities' elections. No state had ever allowed this before.

"The whole country talked about this law. Surprisingly,
Susanna's little city, Argonia, Kansas, became BIG news!"
"What happened?" Ed sprinkled vanilla into the mixing bowl.

It all started two nights before Argonia's election, when Susanna met with a group of women to talk about candidates. They spoke a lot about Mr. S. P. Wilson, who ran the local flour, feed, and coal businesses. Everyone agreed he would make a good mayor, and that his name should be on the election ballot.

"A ballot has the names of people you're voting for, right?" Ed asked.

"Yes," said Dora. "And at the meeting, Susanna and some of the women began planning a sample ballot to give voters on Election Day. It was a list of people they hoped others would vote for too. But just then two men in the back of the room rudely interrupted the meeting."

Ed leaned in.

"They yelled that women should stay out of politics. That they should only raise children, do housework, and..."

"Bake cakes?" Ed asked.

"Yes," Dora said. "But the bullies didn't know Susanna."

Most women at that time couldn't go to college. They didn't learn governing skills.

However, Susanna had done both. And she wanted women's voices heard.

"What did she do?" Ed sprinkled in water.

"Susanna kept working as if the bullies weren't there. The other women followed her lead. They finished writing the ballot."

"Susanna was brave," Ed said.

But Susanna's story wasn't done. (The cake wasn't either!)
"Twenty men from town met in secret and came up with a prank. They made another version of the women's ballot, with one ENORMOUS change..."

"They listed Susanna as candidate for mayor!"

Ed's eyes widened. "I thought those men *didn't* want women voting."

"They didn't!" Dora said. "It was a joke. The bullies believed Susanna could NEVER win. They worried that women would take away their pool halls and saloons. But once Susanna lost, it would prove *nobody* wanted women messing in politics. No woman would ever try again."

"That's mean," Ed huffed.

A group of other men in town didn't like what the bullies did. They brought the new ballot to Susanna's home early in the morning.

Their news stunned her. But their offer shocked her even more.

"The men said they would campaign for Susanna if she agreed to run for mayor—for real!"

"Did these other men honestly want *her* to win?"

Dora nodded. "Yes! If Susanna won, it would teach the bullies that a prank couldn't control Argonia's future. But if she lost, the bullies would win."

"Grandma," Ed said, "why did Susanna take the risk?"

People had wondered that since 1887. Dora knew the answer.

"Susanna felt women had a duty to help shape their cities' futures. She could do that by running for office."

From 8:00 a.m. to 6:00 p.m. on Election Day, Main Street was as busy as a train station, as the people of Argonia campaigned. They held signs. They handed out ballots. They called out their candidates' names.

"Vote for Wilson!"

"Vote for...Susanna?"

And for the first time in Kansas's history, men *and* women were ready to cast their votes!

"I hope Susanna got some votes," Ed said.

"How about two thirds of them?" Dora's eyes twinkled. "Susanna won in a landslide, and Argonians made history. They elected the *world's first woman mayor!*"

When Mayor Susanna served her term, she proved what the bullies feared most. Women could lead a city *and* raise families, run households, and bake cakes—all at the same time.

Finally, the cake was ready.
Ed and his parents gathered around Dora. They sang "Happy Birthday."
One candle flickered on the cake. (Seventy-four couldn't fit.)

Dora made a wish.

"Grandma," Ed said, "did Susanna like being mayor?"

Dora savored the moment. "I felt proud."

Ed stared. "*You?*"

"I started life as a farm girl, then became a college student, wife, pioneer, dressmaker, mother—and your loving grandmother. But to the rest of the world, I'll always be *Mayor Susanna Madora Salter.*"

"Grandmother Mayor!" Ed grinned. "I'm glad you didn't let anybody stop you."

"And I'm glad you helped me bake this cake," said Dora.

"Me too!" said Ed. "It's delicious!"

Author's Note

Susanna Madora "Dora" Salter was born in Ohio in 1860 and grew up on farms in Ohio and Kansas. She attended Kansas State Agricultural College, where she studied dressmaking, leadership, and "parliamentary training." She met her husband, Lewis Salter, there as well, and in 1882 the couple and their baby moved to the new city of Argonia, Kansas.

In 1887, Kansas became the first state to pass a law permitting women to vote and run for office—but only in local elections. Some men in Argonia didn't like this, believing women would make alcohol illegal and close pool halls (and ruin their fun!). They weren't entirely wrong: Salter, like many women across the country, engaged in politics to support prohibition efforts.

At the time, Kansans could announce that they were running for office as late as Election Day. On the morning of Argonia's Election Day, April 4, 1887, twenty men met in secret. According to sources, the "toughest man" present suggested putting Salter on the ballot as a prank and everyone agreed. They wrote up their own version of the women's ballot, but with Salter's name listed as their candidate for mayor. Then they enthusiastically "rushed into the streets and commenced to campaign." Upon seeing his wife's name on the ballot, Lewis begged the men to stop. The bullies simply laughed.

Susanna found out about the prank—and made her historic decision to run for office—while hanging laundry in her yard. She won by a landslide! Salter received two-thirds of the votes—ninety-eight from men and twenty from women. Ultimately, Argonia's men gave Salter her victory.

Three of the bullies won seats on Argonia's city council, which meant they had to follow Salter's lead! Years later, Salter recalled that the council was "kind and courteous" and "there was no discord the entire year."

Argonia's election results made news worldwide. Reporters wrote about Susanna's hairstyle, weight (how would they know?), sewing, and housework. It wasn't until a reporter watched Salter lead a meeting that anyone wrote about her skills as mayor.

After serving a calm one-year term, Salter chose not to run again. But she remained interested in politics and participated in a few suffrage events. The Salters later moved to Oklahoma. Salter enjoyed frontier life, even with its hardships. She fought every challenge, including poverty, to make sure her children received college educations.

Known to her family as "Dora," she celebrated her 101st birthday the same way she always did, by baking an angel food cake! She died later that year, in 1961. Now you can taste a piece of history. Visit www.karengreenwald.com for Dora's secret recipe.

Susanna, young and old

About the Research

For a year and a half, I worked with an incredible stream of dedicated librarians in Ohio and Kansas, historical society genealogists, and Argonians. I delved into the histories of Susanna Salter (or Dora, as I came to know her) and Argonia. Articles from 1887–1890 mainly focus on the election's spectacle. They detail Dora's appearance (often inaccurately) and dishwashing talent. None ponder why she said yes when asked to run for mayor.

This story couldn't have been told without the letters and cards saved by Dora's grandson, Ed Salter. They reveal a sturdy, stubborn, birthday cake baker—a Victorian-born woman, brave enough to risk humiliation, strong enough to raise eight children and run a farm during World War I, yet tender enough to sign letters as "your loving grandmother."

Susanna Salter's history (and that of Argonia) is factually accurate. While it is unclear if she ever baked a cake with Ed, Dora's dialogue in this story is inspired by language used in her letters and those written by Salter family members. Wherever possible, I tried to stay true to her voice and have used her words.

In memory of Ed, and thanks to his children, Mary and David, Dora shared her account of the prank with me—in her own voice, by her own hand. I feel honored to tell her story.

Acknowledgments

Writing this book has been an incredible journey but one I didn't take alone. A special thank you to Mary Roberts-Salter, Carol Wulf Pearce, Valerie Pearce Wade, author Nancy Churnin, and my fantastic editor, Wendy McClure, for helping celebrate Dora. To Brian, Carrie, Joslyn, and my amazing family, thank you for listening to every historic detail and sharing my excitement along the way!